Signs, Wonders and Miracles

The signs of an Apostle

Trevor Newport

New Wine Press

New Wine Press
PO Box 17
Chichester
West Sussex PO20 6YB
England

ISBN 1 903725 38 0

Typeset by CRB Associates, Reepham, Norfolk
Printed in the United States of America

Contents

Foreword

This remarkable book speaks for itself. Trevor Newport, one of today's most highly respected apostles, has given us a document that greatly contributes to building a solid foundation under what I like to call the New Apostolic Reformation.

First of all, my friend Apostle Newport has scoured the Scriptures for the passages relevant to authenticating the gift and office of apostle. If the idea of true, New Testament-type apostles today could not be substantiated from the Bible, he would be among the first to reject the idea.

Secondly, Trevor brings to those scriptures an enviable track record of international ministry that provides him the maturity and experience to interpret those scriptures for the rest of us in a way that helps open our ears to hear what the Spirit is saying to the churches these days.

Let me tell you why I think that this book that you have in your hands is important for all of us who, not only are believers in Christ, but who also want to be among those whom God is using on the cutting edge of the history-making changes that He is bringing to the church and also to the world in these days.

Important for the Church
The fact that apostles are here to stay is important for the Church. A huge historical milestone came with the

Protestant Reformation in the sixteenth century. We absolutely had to understand that justification came through faith if we were to move ahead. Another milestone came with William Carey's Enquiry which opened the doors for the modern missionary movement. That was a little over two hundred years ago, and the progress in world evangelization made since then is a remarkable phenomenon. A third significant milestone was the advent of the Pentecostal Movement about one hundred years ago when the person and the work of the Holy Spirit began to be widely recognized.

I mention these three milestones of Church history because this book helps tune us into a new development for the Church which is at least as important as any of them, namely the rediscovery of the true government of the Church. The Church, according to the New Testament, is founded on apostles and prophets (see Ephesians 2:20). In fact Paul says that God gave to the Church first apostles (see 1 Corinthians 12:28). Now that we are getting the government of the Church in its proper order, we can expect to see much greater spiritual power manifested in the Body of Christ than we have ever known.

Important for Society

But recognizing the gift and office of apostle is not only important for the Church, it is also important for our society. One of the changes that is accompanying the New Apostolic Reformation is that God's people are now focusing not only on saving souls and planting churches and feeding the poor, but also on transforming society. The prayer that Jesus taught us, 'Your kingdom come, Your will be done on earth as it is in heaven,' is being taken more seriously than it has in generations. Why would this be true?

I think the answer is quite simple. Satan, as the god of this age, has been maintaining his domination of society for much too long. One thing that enables him to do this is that he has a government. This has given him an advantage over the Church for centuries. How can this be changed? It takes a government to overthrow a government. Satan has now more than met his match. The Church is now ready to move with great power because its biblical government is coming into place. It is a government that begins with apostles.

Apostles are not only here to stay, they are here to make war and they are here to conquer the enemy. They are here to move the Church into its destiny and to transform society for the glory of the Father!

If you want to be a part of this tremendously exciting move of God, nothing could be more important than reading and digesting the contents of this book!

C. Peter Wagner
Presiding Apostle
International Coalition of Apostles

Chapter 1

Restoration of the Five-fold Ministries

Let us look at the Bible passage dealing with the ministry gifts:

> *'And he gave some, apostles; and some, prophets; and some, evangelists; and some, pastors and teachers;*
>
> *For the perfecting of the saints, for the work of the ministry, for the edifying of the body of Christ:*
>
> *Till we all come in the unity of the faith, and of the knowledge of the Son of God, unto a perfect man, unto the measure of the stature of the fulness of Christ.'*
>
> (Ephesians 4:11–13)

Notice first of all that this does not say that those in ministry are to do the work of the ministry. It says that those in ministry are to perfect the saints to do the work of ministry! How many leaders have missed that one? Our job is to do ourselves out of a job by reproducing our gifts into carefully chosen people who will continue and grow in their calling allowing us to move into the next step of what God has for us. This causes everyone to be fulfilled and to get the chance to grow in ministry.

Over the last few decades something has been happening throughout the whole Body of Christ in relation to the five-fold ministries. Not only has the Holy Spirit brought different waves and moves at certain times but He has also been busy at restoring the above ministries in just about every part of the Church.

For instance, during the 1950s and 1960s there was a major move of God all over the world of healing evangelists. Multitudes of people came to Christ. Tents and huge auditoriums were filled to hear and see different evangelists preach the gospel with signs and wonders following. I believe that this was part of God's plan to begin the work of restoring His ministries back to the Church. At least, those who would embrace them.

I think that we all agree that the ministry gift of pastor is essential in the Church and it is the most comfortable title for most church leaders.

Then, during the 1970s and 1980s there was shift of emphasis as the ministry gift of the teacher was restored largely due to the Word of Faith movement, along with others. Bible teachers started springing up all over the place and conferences for teaching became the norm.

Then during the end of the 1980s and particularly during the 1990s there was so much talk about prophets and the ministry of the prophetic. God was restoring this wonderful gift back to the Church. Even many who were involved in teaching began to move in the prophetic. That is the best way round. Personally, I believe that it is better to have a good foundation of the Word of God before activating the prophetic. It saves a lot of cleaning up afterwards!

The final ministry gift is that of the apostle. I believe that God is in the process right at this time (2004) of restoring the office of apostle back to the Church in preparation for a move of God to take our cities for Jesus before His return.

Like an enormous game of chess, the pieces have to be placed strategically in preparation for the final showdown against the enemy!

Thus, all five ministry gifts must be in place to deal with the devil.

Chapter 2

The Weight of Scripture Regarding Apostles

Let me ask you a question. How many times do you think that the word 'pastor' or 'pastors' is used in the New Testament? It gets used all the time in many churches. Can I speak to the pastor please? Oh pastor, I need an appointment etc. It is so set in people's minds throughout the world. Let us get back to my initial question. If you look at the frequency to which it is used you would think that pastor appeared hundreds of times in the New Testament. You would be very wrong. In fact, it is only used once, and that is in the plural in Ephesians 4:11.

However, how often do you hear someone ask for Apostle Peter, or Apostle John?

I am going to shock some of you now by telling you how many times the term 'apostle' or 'apostles' is mentioned in the New Testament. Have a guess yourself. Now I will tell you. The term 'apostle' is used nineteen times and the term 'apostles' is used sixty times! Seventy-nine times in total as opposed to one reference to pastor. What happened to us? Who shifted the balance? Who is responsible for majoring on pastors instead of apostles? This has got to change! You may be interested to know how many times the other giftings are mentioned. Evangelist or evangelists is mentioned three times, teacher or teachers is mentioned thirteen

11

times and there are 150 references to prophets. Surely, apostles and prophets should have a much higher profile and recognition than the other ministries instead of the other way round! Pray for this change to come in line with this biblical precedent.

Let us look at another aspect of this from what Paul has to say:

> '*And God hath set some in the church, **first** apostles, **secondarily** prophets, thirdly teachers, after that miracles, then gifts of healings, helps, governments, diversities of tongues.*'   (1 Corinthians 12:28, emphasis added)

I have just looked up the word 'first' in the Greek dictionary and it means 'firstly in time, place or order of importance'. Also, it means 'before all else, at the start, chiefly and first of all'. Just meditate on that for a while! I think we need apostles! We need them to rise up and take their rightful place in the Kingdom.

How can we have missed something so fundamental for so long?

Chapter 3

How I Was Called into Apostolic Ministry

I answered the call of God upon my life when I was very young. I was twenty-one years old. I had become a Christian at nineteen through a young man called Brian who witnessed to me constantly for about nine months at which time I had the most radical conversion from a very worldly life. I shared Jesus with hundreds of people and devoured the Bible spending hours a day reading and studying it.

After a year I received the baptism in the Holy Spirit and spoke in tongues. Very soon after this experience I knew that God was calling me into full-time service for Him. I told Him that I was far too young and that I wanted to complete my university studies, get married, get a house, car etc. and then I would serve Him. He told me that He wanted me before I got anything! I obeyed and gave up my career and security and embarked on a life of faith. I have never looked back and I have never regretted taking that step of faith.

Anyway, I found myself pastor of a small Pentecostal church in Liverpool where I started my ministry. I soon realised how much I did not know! I am so glad that I had an overseer that I went to for three hours every two weeks so that I could pick his brains! His name was Aubrey Whittall. He was the senior minister of the Liverpool Elim church. He was brilliant for me because he had been in ministry for decades and moved in healing, deliverance, prophecy etc. It was the best Bible college I could have had.

As I began ministering all those years ago I noticed that the teaching gift started to unfold and become very strong upon me. If ever I tried to preach an evangelistic message I would end up teaching believers! That was the first ministry gift to be realised in my life. I soon became quite confident and comfortable in teaching and loved to teach about five times a week. I also realised that too much study on one subject would end up becoming a series of messages.

Then the pastoral anointing began to ignite and I would preach messages that would home in on people where they were at. So, each time I spoke it would either be pastoral or teaching or a bit of both. I thought that that would be it! I knew that I was called to lead a church and was very happy doing it.

Then, after a few years, a new anointing started to manifest! I did not recognise it at first but later realised that it was the office of the prophet. My pastor had told me to expect it at some time and sure enough it did! I would prepare a teaching message and the Holy Spirit would lead me in a completely different direction. Afterwards people would come up to me and say that when I went off at a tangent that it was just for them. That is one aspect of prophetic preaching. I was very uncomfortable to start with and would try to step back into teaching but the Holy Spirit kept doing it to the point where I was confident in all three giftings.

Throughout my ministry the one gifting that is the least used in me is the evangelist anointing, though I do see people come to know Christ. In the last twelve years I have seen about 12,000 decisions for Jesus in all the meetings that I have ministered at.

I had told the Lord all through the early years of ministry that I never wanted to write a book, I never wanted to travel overseas (particularly to the USA), and I definitely did not want to be an apostle! In 1992 I was fasting and praying and God told me three things that totally shocked me! Firstly, write a book, secondly, go to the USA and thirdly, 'I have called you to be an apostle, please accept this calling.' I was shellshocked for days. I had failed English language at school three times before finally passing and my teacher always used to put a big red line through my essays and say that it was gobbledegook! I did maths at school and ended up coming top and taking the prize at a school that usually had at least eighteen candidates for Oxford and Cambridge.

So writing was not my strong point. It was my weakest. Anyway, I wrote my first booklet. It took me six months and I produced twenty-four pages. That was nineteen books ago! In fact, the ministry has developed more through my books than any other aspect of ministry. The pen is mightier that the sword!

In 1993 I flew to Los Angeles by faith with no appointments to speak, very little money in my pocket, no hotels booked and I did not know anybody! God told me to go and I ended up staying in Southern California and ministered to several people. That was the start of my international travelling. I have since been to the USA twenty-six times to preach as well as fifty-nine other countries.

However, the third thing that God had said to me was the hardest to take in: 'I have called you to be an apostle, please accept the call.' I resisted this word from God for three years. I wanted to be completely sure in my heart that this was God Himself. I had never wanted this ministry, never asked for it. In fact I had publicly said years before that I would never call myself an apostle. The following scriptures had made me over-cautious of this gift:

'For such are false apostles, deceitful workers, transforming themselves into the apostles of Christ.'

(2 Corinthians 11:13)

'I know thy works, and thy labour, and thy patience, and how thou canst not bear them which are evil: and thou hast tried them which say they are apostles, and are not, and hast found them liars.'   (Revelation 2:2)

I never wanted to be found as a false apostle, self-anointed and puffed up by my own ego! What good would that do for the Kingdom? I would rather go and earn an honest salary doing a secular job and serve God in my vocation.

After three years of resisting the apostolic call I finally accepted it but did not know what was going to happen. I was leading a small church which was still in its pioneer stage. Nobody had ever come up to me and asked if they could be covered by me spiritually.

The next chapter will tell you what happened straight after I accepted it.

Chapter 4

My Personal Visit from Jesus Christ

Two weeks after I had accepted the apostolic call I was sitting in our prayer room along with Ruth and our children and four others. We were praying together for about two hours before our deliverance school. All of a sudden the presence of God came into the room and rendered all eight of us out in the Spirit. We could not move a muscle, only our eyes. My wife looked at me with her piercing eyes as if to say, 'What have you done now?' We were motionless for about five minutes when something happened that was awesome. I saw heaven begin to open and three angels come down with Jesus in the middle of them. They all walked along our corridor and the three angels stayed outside the prayer room. Jesus came into the prayer meeting and walked straight up to me with a big beaming smile on His face. I did not know what was happening. Jesus then proceeded to slap me heartily on my shoulder and He said these words: 'Hi Trev, it's your brother Jesus here. I have just come to tell you that your ministry is just about to start. Bye!'

I was in a state of shock for a few minutes as I watched Jesus join the angels and go back to heaven with extreme joy on all of their faces.

After a few minutes the presence of God lifted off us and we were able to move. From that moment people began to enquire about joining our ministry and coming under my apostolic covering, even though I had told nobody about what had taken place! I did not advertise anywhere about this apostolic office. It was all new to us. I was thirty-five years old when I finally accepted it. I also had five visits from angels – all in my bedroom – after that visit from Jesus. By the way, it was not a vision of Jesus. He was actually there in our prayer room. When He slapped my arm I felt it and physically moved. I have seen Him twice since but both times were in visions. I have only seen Him once in reality.

A new anointing came upon me in every area of ministry. Churches and ministries started asking about covering and we now have ministries in England, Wales, Sri Lanka, Nepal, India, Colorado, Nigeria, Zambia and Cameroon with other applications coming in regularly. God spoke to me and said that our church would become a headquarters and mother church to many, which has come to pass.

Chapter 5

Paul the Apostle

It is very interesting how Paul begins virtually all of his epistles:

> *'Paul, a servant of Jesus Christ, called to be an apostle, separated unto the gospel of God.'* (Romans 1:1)

> *'Paul, called to be an apostle of Jesus Christ through the will of God, and Sosthenes our brother.'* (1 Corinthians 1:1)

Notice he says in these initial letters *'called to be an apostle'*. Just see what he says after these initial two epistles:

> *'Paul, an apostle of Jesus Christ by the will of God, and Timothy our brother, unto the church of God which is at Corinth, with all the saints which are in all Achaia.'* (2 Corinthians 1:1)

> *'Paul, an apostle, (not of men, neither by man, but by Jesus Christ, and God the Father, who raised him from the dead).'* (Galatians 1:1)

> *'Paul, an apostle of Jesus Christ by the will of God, to the saints which are at Ephesus, and to the faithful in Christ Jesus.'* (Ephesians 1:1)

19

> *'Paul, an apostle of Jesus Christ by the will of God, and Timotheus our brother.'*   (Colossians 1:1)

> *'Paul, an apostle of Jesus Christ by the commandment of God our Saviour, and Lord Jesus Christ, which is our hope.'*
> (1 Timothy 1:1)

> *'Paul, an apostle of Jesus Christ by the will of God, according to the promise of life which is in Christ Jesus.'*
> (2 Timothy 1:1)

It is as if he has accepted the office of an apostle and is getting used to it! He makes reference to the apostolic in most of his epistles including Titus:

> *'Paul, a servant of God, and an apostle of Jesus Christ, according to the faith of God's elect, and the acknowledging of the truth which is after godliness.'*   (Titus 1:1)

Both of Peter's epistles also refer to his own apostleship:

> *'Peter, an apostle of Jesus Christ, to the strangers scattered throughout Pontus, Galatia, Cappadocia, Asia, and Bithynia.'*   (1 Peter 1:1)

> *'Simon Peter, a servant and an apostle of Jesus Christ, to them that have obtained like precious faith with us through the righteousness of God and our Saviour Jesus Christ.'*
> (2 Peter 1:1)

Thus both Paul and Peter recognised their calling as apostles and were not frightened or intimidated to use the title frequently.

Chapter 6

What Is an Apostle?

The Strong's definition of an apostle is:

'A delegate; specially an ambassador of the gospel; officially a commissioner of Christ with miraculous powers; he that is sent.'

An apostle is like a plough that opens up new ground and territory for the gospel. Others have to come in afterwards and tend to that newly ploughed up ground but it needs the apostle to first plough it up!

Many missionaries who went into foreign lands to reach people who had never heard the gospel were functioning as apostles by this definition. They were often used by God to demonstrate the gospel with signs and wonders, to convince the people that Jesus Christ was greater than their pagan gods. I once remember being told the story of such a missionary who went into a country where the language had never been translated before. The missionaries learned the language and began to share Jesus Christ with them. Nothing happened at all. None of the native people responded to the gospel, until one day, years later the whole village came to Christ in a single day! The missionaries were baffled and asked the people what had happened. They said that it was not the preaching that had convinced them to accept Jesus but the fact that in the last few years they had been poisoning the missionaries with extremely venomous poison that would have killed several elephants, let alone human beings! They realised that Jesus Christ must be much greater than their pagan gods since Jesus had protected the missionaries from the poison. Hallelujah!

An apostle is a trailblazer for others to follow. You could use the term 'pioneer', someone called to initiate something new in the Kingdom of God. John G. Lake was sent by the Holy Spirit to go to Cape Town in South Africa with many children. God had provided for him by showing a lady that he was coming. This lady had a home just the right size to look after Lake and his large family. He pioneered hundreds of churches which are still going strong to this day after 100 years. That is the ministry of the apostle!

An apostle is also likened to the thumb on your hand. The thumb can touch all four fingers. An apostle is a mix of two, three or four of the other ministry gifts. An apostle is also able to minister to the other four ministry gifts to impart, instruct and advise.

An apostle is able to see with the eye of faith into the future as a visionary and usually has an extraordinary deposit of faith to complete his tasks.

Chapter 7

The Signs of an Apostle

Some of the ingredients of a true New Testament apostle are signs, wonders, healings and miracles.

> '*Truly the signs of an apostle were wrought among you in all patience, in signs, and wonders, and mighty deeds.*'   (2 Corinthians 12:12, emphasis added)

A track record of miracles is essential if we claim to be a true apostle. I have personally experienced countless miracles of healing, deliverances from demons, financial miracles, recreative miracles, prophetic miracles etc.

Even the early disciples of Jesus who became apostles were used to seeing miracles and they were not yet born again and certainly not Spirit filled!

> '*Then he called his twelve disciples together, and gave them power and authority over all devils, and to cure diseases.*
>
> *And he sent them to preach the kingdom of God, and to heal the sick.*'   (Luke 9:1–2)

> '*And they departed, and went through the towns, preaching the gospel, and healing every where.*'   (Luke 9:6)

'And the apostles, when they were returned, told him all that they had done. And he took them, and went aside privately into a desert place belonging to the city called Bethsaida.'

(Luke 9:10)

In my experience of the miraculous power of God I see many more mighty miracles when I travel than when I stay at home. Particularly when I travel overseas. It is as if the anointing is much greater upon me. I have come to realise the words of Jesus when He said this:

'For Jesus himself testified, that a prophet hath no honour in his own country.'   (John 4:44)

I have shared with many about this point regarding the miraculous and most are in agreement. Just watch what happens the first time that you travel! I can often feel the anointing coming upon me a few days before I set off again and many times on the flight I can feel the signs and wonders anointing getting me ready for multiple show-downs with the works of the devil! I am just having a book published called *Present-Day Miracles* which tells of forty special miracles that have happened in my life and ministry.

Chapter 8

What Does an Apostle Do?

There are different types of apostles who do varying tasks in the kingdom and we shall deal with the differences in a later chapter.

First, an apostle must develop a very close and personal relationship with the Father and be able to hear clearly what the Holy Spirit is saying. This involves time out of a busy schedule so that he can spend quality time listening to the voice of the Lord. Over the past twelve years I have gone to a retreat house for about four days for at least three times a year to check out our vision and make sure that we were on track. I would spend a few days just praying in the Spirit and seeking the heart of God. Often He would give me a long list of things to do when I got back.

I remember one time I was away and seeking God for three days and He said nothing to me. I was beginning to wonder if something was wrong. Then the familiar voice of the Holy Spirit said to me these words: 'You are doing everything that I have told you to do and are in the right mode to hear My voice; just keep doing what you are doing.' Usually I would return home with a long list of things to do but this time I could feel the pleasure of the Lord knowing that I was in His perfect will and doing everything that He wanted of me. I still spend time just seeking His face from time to time but I do find that I am hearing His voice more clearly these days than ever before. I must be growing up!

Many years ago I was challenged by this scripture from the Old Testament:

> *'(Now the man Moses was very meek, above all the men which were upon the face of the earth.)*
>
> *And the* Lord *spake suddenly unto Moses, and unto Aaron, and unto Miriam, Come out ye three unto the tabernacle of the congregation. And they three came out.*
>
> *And the* Lord *came down in the pillar of the cloud, and stood in the door of the tabernacle, and called Aaron and Miriam: and they both came forth.*
>
> *And he said, Hear now my words: If there be a prophet among you, I the* Lord *will make myself known unto him in a vision, and will speak unto him in a dream.*
>
> ***My servant Moses is not so, who is faithful in all mine house.***
>
> ***With him will I speak mouth to mouth, even apparently, and not in dark speeches;*** *and the similitude of the* Lord *shall he behold: wherefore then were ye not afraid to speak against my servant Moses?'*
>
> (Numbers 12:3–8, emphasis added)

I believe that an apostle has this kind of relationship with God whereby he can hear from God directly. I know that many rely on the prophetic voice to guide their steps and I am not saying that that is wrong. However, I would say that when God speaks to your spirit it is a primary word. When a prophet speaks to you it is a secondary word. I have had prophets who have confirmed what God has said to me from time to time but I have also had prophets who have tried to lead me astray from what God has said to me. I have come to the conclusion that when someone prophesies to me it has to be accompanied with an inward witness from the Holy Spirit as they are speaking or else I reject it straight away.

We need to make sure that a prophetic word is not a pathetic word! I have had plenty of those over the years! In fact I kept count of personal words given to me over the years and I may shock you when I tell you that out of 170 prophetic words given to me in twenty-three years only eight of those words were from God!

The next thing that an apostle must do is to build a team – particularly if you are away regularly. It takes time to build a team around you and can be very painful at times but the secret about building a team is 'never give up'. I now have an excellent team around me who are the most dedicated and committed people who I trust with all my heart. However, it has taken thirteen years to build it!

My wife Ruth, who heads up the team, is the finest person I have ever worked with. When we started our church thirteen years ago we had hardly anybody who could take responsibility of any sort. After just two years of pioneering the Lord moved upon me to start travelling around the world. I asked Him, 'Who is going to look after the church while I am gone?' The Lord replied and said 'Ruth will take charge.' I then said to God, 'Would You please tell her then?' He said 'No! You tell her and I will confirm to her.' That is how my wife began her ministry. She is now the senior pastor of the mother church of Life Changing Ministries and doing a great job!

The next thing that is absolutely imperative is to raise up an army of intercessors. I cannot emphasise this point enough. You need strong warriors praying at all times. Let me give you an example. Last Sunday one of my main intercessors came up to me and said that she was going to be fasting and praying for me this week while I was writing this book. That makes all the difference. You see, she can be praying things off me without me even being aware. That is the job of intercessors, to pray protection around us so that we can do our job. Also to engage in warfare where needed. I produce a prayer letter letting all of my intercessors know where I am and what I am doing. I can often feel the prayer support when I am travelling, flying or writing.

'Brethren, pray for us.'   (1 Thessalonians 5:25)

'Finally, brethren, pray for us, that the word of the Lord may have free course, and be glorified, even as it is with you.'
          (2 Thessalonians 3:1)

'Pray for us: for we trust we have a good conscience, in all things willing to live honestly.'   (Hebrews 13:18)

An apostle breaks into new territory and births new things on the earth. An apostle also helps others to fulfil their destiny and vision. This has been a great joy for me over the last few years as people with vision have come to me and I have been able to release them into their calling, often by helping them to get started in a new church for instance. Thus an apostle must be able to recognise the gifting and calling upon others and have the authority to release that gifting. This is multiplication. In our apostolic network of churches we have those that I have released and also those who have contacted us who already have a church or churches seeking a covering. Many who have joined our network have experienced much blessing and growth, and the provision of larger buildings. It has been a joy to watch God at work.

Chapter 9

Do We Need Apostles Today?

I believe that we need apostles today more than ever before. Firstly, we need apostles to complete the restoration of the five-fold gifts back to the Church. How can we expect to have the fullness of revival for our cities without all five ministry gifts working in harmony? Independent churches that do not have apostolic covering need to seek out an apostle that they can relate to and join a network that is fulfilling present-day Christianity.

We need apostles today to provide fatherly support to leaders who have nobody to watch over them. An apostle can give guidance, direction, input, strength, agreement of vision, as well as personal pastoral help.

I strongly believe that the great commission will not be fulfilled without apostles taking their rightful place in preparation for the coming move of God.

We always need apostles in any age to offer covering, to impart giftings, release signs and wonders and to complete the perfecting of the saints for the work of ministry. Pastors and teachers alone cannot fully perfect the saints for the work of ministry. We need all five gifts working together to produce strong Christians who can reproduce themselves and bring the unsaved to Christ.

If ever the Church of Jesus Christ needed apostles it is now more than ever. I challenge you to pray right now for those who are being called into apostolic ministry to have the courage to take their place and to accept this calling. This is completely unselfish on their part, as it will increase their workload significantly as they find their sphere of influence widening tremendously. It will certainly have an impact on other branches of the Kingdom of God, which comes with the apostolic gift.

Chapter 10

Different Areas of Authority

Every apostle needs to realise that they only have authority in certain places. When I am in my local church I have permanent authority and everybody recognises that authority without me having to enforce it all the time. However, when I travel to someone else's church I only have temporal authority which is given to me while I am ministering. When I leave then my authority lifts in that place.

Another aspect of authority is to do with a city. Some apostles have authority within their own city but nowhere else in particular. We need to identify where our authority is and to submit to others where our authority ceases.

Often when I am in a different country an apostle will literally delegate his authority to me for the duration of my time in his territory, as I have often done when we have apostles into our ministry.

The Holy Spirit will often tell me to go to a certain country before I get an invitation to the country. Therefore, when I am invited I know that my authority will be recognised without striving at all. I believe that this is being sent. In the last few years I have been to Colombia six times and have ministered in most of the cities in that wonderful country. However, it was about four years earlier that the Lord spoke to me and said that one day He would open the door for me to minister in Colombia. It was only when the door was actually opened that my apostolic authority was recognised.

This has happened in many countries around the globe over the last eleven years. I went to Australia for five consecutive years because the Holy Spirit had told me to go and then the door opened up for me through one of my books. I thus knew that my authority would be recognised, which it was. I saw some outstanding apostolic signs and wonders in those five trips down under. Then that season of my ministry lifted and I stopped going and other countries opened up for me.

I want to give you a wonderful example from a mighty man of God called Ulf Ekman. God had used Ulf Ekman to pioneer a powerful church in Uppsala, Sweden, which grew to about 2,000 members. Then God spoke to Ulf and told him to hire a train from a KGB agent in Russia and take it right through Russia with gospel literature, books, tapes and videos etc. He obeyed and ended up planting hundreds of churches throughout Russia as well as a Bible School in Moscow. God gave Ulf a command which gave Ulf authority to go and do what He had said. I remember praying when I was in Sweden and asked the Lord about how He had been able to do so much through one man. God answered me with these words: 'The only difference between you and Ulf Ekman is ten years.' I said, 'What does that mean?' God said to me that if I obey Him as Ulf has obeyed Him then I would see the same results! I was so encouraged by that.

Obedience is the key to the level of success that we shall see in any aspect of ministry. I have determined to obey the Lord in everything because I want to see maximum fruit. Look what God said to Abraham:

> '*And the angel of the* Lord *called unto Abraham out of heaven the second time,*
> *And said, By myself have I sworn, saith the* Lord, *for because thou hast done this thing, and hast not withheld thy son, thine only son:*

That in blessing I will bless thee, and in multiplying I will multiply thy seed as the stars of the heaven, *and as the sand which is upon the sea shore; and thy seed shall possess the gate of his enemies;*

And in thy seed shall all the nations of the earth be blessed; because thou hast obeyed my voice.'

(Genesis 22:15–18, emphasis added)

If we want our ministry to increase and multiply then all we have to do is to obey the voice of the Lord without any compromise and we shall see great things accomplished through our lives.

Chapter 11

The Accountability of an Apostle

We all need accountability and covering in our lives, who-
ever we are. When I was first in ministry I came under the
wise counsel of a very godly man who was my pastor,
Aubrey Whittall. He continued to be my mentor, advisor
and covering for twenty years until he died and went to be
with the Lord. He was so full of wisdom and knowledge and I
would spend hours on the telephone with him and we
would talk about all sorts of subjects. It was the best thing
for a young pastor to have someone to be able to go to about
literally anything. I also spent several years going to his
home once every two weeks for three hour sessions to talk
about doctrine, pastoral issues, miracles, deliverance etc. He
was full of stories that had happened to him over his many
decades of ministry.

We built up a real relationship which is the basis for any
true covering. I have observed many people trying to cover
people where there is no real relationship. I call this admin-
istrative covering. This does not work since you would never
seek help on personal issues with someone who you could
not trust or have any relationship with. I believe that all true
covering comes out of relationship. I would not be in
ministry today without the help of my pastor.

Thus when he went to be with the Lord I was faced with
having to replace Aubrey with someone else. Firstly, I made
quality relationships with a few guys in my city who all

speak into my life. Also, my precious wife who has grown very much in ministry speaks often into my life. The Holy Spirit regularly speaks to me about things also, which is part of my accountability. However, I knew that I wanted more and prayed to the Father about joining with other apostles with whom I could develop relationships. I did not know any but when I was in Bogota preaching in Colombia one year my friend Hector Pardoe mentioned to me about the International Coalition of Apostles with C. Peter Wagner. I said that I had never heard about it and so he gave me an application form. However, it was in Spanish! So when I got home I e-mailed Dr Wagner to ask for a form in English and I had a reply that said that Peter did not know me and would I send a full account of my ministry etc. I thought that I was striving and so decided to forget the idea!

I went off on another international trip preaching in different countries and while I was away the Holy Spirit told me to pursue the International Coalition of Apostles. So I decided that when I went home that I would send all that Peter had asked for. When I got home I had a pleasant surprise! Dr Wagner had written a personal letter to me inviting me to become a member of ICA without any need of any further information. I was intrigued. Peter went on to say that he had done some checking about my ministry and was convinced that I was a true apostle. I could not imagine who had spoken up for me but was quite shocked as well as very pleased. So I became a member of ICA from January 2001. I have attended each annual conference in Dallas with apostles from all over the world and it has been the source of great blessing and mutual strength. Even though ICA is not directly a covering it does give a secondary accountability by being at the conference. Also, I have built some wonderful relationships with senior apostles who I can look up to and receive help from. I have also asked one in particular to be my personal covering to replace my dear pastor Aubrey.

The greater our responsibility in the Kingdom the stronger our covering needs to be.

Another aspect of covering is intercessors. The ones who pray for us are really helping to form part of our covering and protection which we need so very much. If you do not have strong prayer warriors around you then train some up and give some instruction on how to pray for you. This is essential for any apostle doing this kind of trailblazing!

That is all to do with spiritual accountability. We also need financial accountability. Since I am still part of a local church and preside over Life Changing Ministries I liase with our church accountant on a regular basis on financial issues. Also, I have my own accountant to whom I have to give an annual report for tax purposes. That was a blessing from God since she hardly charges me for her services and she is not even a believer but she is brilliant and knows all of the tax saving rules.

'Obey them that have the rule over you, and submit yourselves: for they watch for your souls, as they that must give account, that they may do it with joy, and not with grief: for that is unprofitable for you.'   (Hebrews 13:17)

Chapter 12

Apostolic Persecution

'Therefore I take pleasure in infirmities, in reproaches, in necessities, in persecutions, in distresses for Christ's sake: for when I am weak, then am I strong.' (2 Corinthians 12:10)

'But thou hast fully known my doctrine, manner of life, purpose, faith, longsuffering, charity, patience,

Persecutions, afflictions, which came unto me at Antioch, at Iconium, at Lystra; what persecutions I endured: but out of them all the Lord delivered me.' (2 Timothy 3:10–11)

'Are they ministers of Christ? (I speak as a fool) I am more; in labours more abundant, in stripes above measure, in prisons more frequent, in deaths oft.

Of the Jews five times received I forty stripes save one.

Thrice was I beaten with rods, once was I stoned, thrice I suffered shipwreck, a night and a day I have been in the deep;

In journeyings often, in perils of waters, in perils of robbers, in perils by mine own countrymen, in perils by the heathen, in perils in the city, in perils in the wilderness, in perils in the sea, in perils among false brethren;

In weariness and painfulness, in watchings often, in hunger and thirst, in fastings often, in cold and nakedness.

Beside those things that are without, that which cometh upon me daily, the care of all the churches.'

(2 Corinthians 11:23–28)

Paul certainly knew what suffering for the gospel meant! However, the Lord had warned him at the point of his calling:

> *'But the Lord said unto him, Go thy way: for he is a chosen vessel unto me, to bear my name before the Gentiles, and kings, and the children of Israel:*
> *For I will shew him how great things he must suffer for my name's sake.'*   (Acts 9:15–16)

I have read the New Testament many times and am very aware of the sufferings attached to the apostolic. That is one of the reasons why I did not want the job. To be honest, I had had enough trials, attacks and problems being a pastor let alone an apostle!

Anyway, when we began our church in the centre of our city in Stoke on Trent, England, all hell broke loose! My name was mud for years! People kept telling me about letters that were being sent around the churches telling people not to have anything to do with me. I was really popular! I was accused of all sorts of things. Then a big letter appeared in our main newspaper in the city by a jezebel lady that I had disciplined. Then we had a season of five jezebel ladies that came to our church to cause as much trouble as they could. We ended up with the conclusion that the only way to deal with Jezebel is to have zero tolerance.

Then we had so many problems with leaders that we tried to help to release. They kept turning against me!

We also had a season of territorial warfare in the spirit realm. When we moved into our HQ building about ten years ago the people who were decorating it heard strange noises and smelt funny smells while they were working. So we went to pray and God showed me that a destroying spirit had been assigned to our church to destroy us, called Apollyon. So I took one of our guys who was a prophet with me and we spent all night in prayer until the destroyer showed up. I saw him coming down our corridor to torment us. I could see him which is a great advantage! I spoke to him and gave him his marching orders. He left in terror. After that time people began to report angels in our building.

Then another attack happened against me that lasted for two years. We were living by faith and trusting God for money all the time as we had been doing for the previous fifteen years. Each day when I got up the devil would attack me and tell me to go and get a job. He was relentless and jobs would jump out of adverts and the devil would say that I could earn a fortune as well as lead the ministry. It was very tempting but I resisted it again and again. Then the word of the Lord came to me and said that God was going to bless me more for staying in ministry and fulfilling His purpose than any job I could do in the world. I can honestly say that God has kept His word to me, as I am such a blessed man.

So, persecution comes with the territory of being an apostle. Also, on my international trips I have almost been killed on three occasions that I know about! I once had 500 Hamas trying to kill me for helping to take a crusade in Bethlehem. On another occasion I was asked to open a church in a strictly Hindu village on the outskirts of Madras, India. The militant Hindus had promised to kill the man from England if I went ahead and opened it. I did not know that this was all going on and at the end of the service I was loaded into a car and we drove off at high speed. Then they told me that I had been given a death threat! God has protected me and delivered me from all kinds of dangers out on the mission field.

I have come through all of that much stronger in my faith and much more in love with Jesus Christ as a result. It is part of the refining process. Hallelujah!

'Who delivered us from so great a death, and doth deliver: in whom we trust that he will yet deliver us.'

(2 Corinthians 1:10)

'And the Lord shall deliver me from every evil work, and will preserve me unto his heavenly kingdom: to whom be glory for ever and ever. Amen.' (2 Timothy 4:18)

'The Lord knoweth how to deliver the godly out of temptations, and to reserve the unjust unto the day of judgment to be punished.' (2 Peter 2:9)

I know many who have left the ministry because of the sufferings they have had to endure. But I can report that it has been worth suffering for His Name's sake to be counted worthy to suffer like the early apostles I read of in Acts 5:40–41:

'And to him they agreed: and when they had called the apostles, and beaten them, they commanded that they should not speak in the name of Jesus, and let them go.

And they departed from the presence of the council, rejoicing that they were counted worthy to suffer shame for his name.'

Another aspect of apostolic suffering is that some people that we have helped a great deal have turned against us. This has happened several times in my ministry and I am sure it happens in every apostolic camp! Look what Paul says:

'Alexander the coppersmith did me much evil: the Lord reward him according to his works:

Of whom be thou ware also; for he hath greatly withstood our words.

At my first answer no man stood with me, but all men forsook me: I pray God that it may not be laid to their charge.

*Notwithstanding the Lord stood with me, and strength-
ened me; that by me the preaching might be fully known, and
that all the Gentiles might hear: and I was delivered out of
the mouth of the lion.'*   (2 Timothy 4:14–17)

We all have to cope with rejection and be healed of it so that
we will trust again and help others to fulfil their destiny.

Chapter 13

Apostolic Praying and Warfare

I believe that every apostle has a unique mandate from the Father to complete. For some it can start off locally in your own town or city. It can then unfold into your region and then country. It can also become continental or even global. You must follow what the Holy Spirit says to you and complete the tasks given by Him.

I began praying fervently for my own city as directed by the Lord. This involved much intercession and spiritual warfare in the heavenlies since worship was very difficult when we first started. It was a continual battleground. We would often have to stop and war against territorial spirits before we could even worship. This went on for many years since our city was a place of almost total darkness.

God had told me to take this territory and to take the centre of the city. After a few years we noticed that things slowly started to change in the heavenly realm and small breakthroughs began. The Lord also told me to specifically pray for all of the churches to come together and to work together for where there is unity then the Lord commands the blessing. I acquired the names of every church and leader in our city and our whole church went to prayer. Historically, the Christian leaders of our city have found it very difficult to work together even though many attempts had been made. About three years ago an amazing break-through took place. All of a sudden there was an awareness among church leaders that we needed to work and pray together which resulted in a city-wide prayer gathering once a month along with leaders' meetings. It took seven years but it has been worth it. Many are now looking for a city transformation. I also believe that this has been the desire of many in our city.

Once we had dealt with the main stronghold over our city, the Lord then led me to go to other cities to do the same. I obeyed Him and went into Paris, Brussels, Berlin, Bern and other cities in Europe. I usually went with Peter the prophet who was a great travelling companion. Then the Lord sent me further afield to the USA, South America, Russia, India, Sri Lanka, China, Singapore, Australia, South Africa, Bermuda, Jamaica, Israel, Japan and many other places. One day, on the TGV high-speed train from Paris to Geneva the Spirit of God spoke to me and said that He was going to send me to every major capital city in the world to engage in spiritual warfare. Over the next ten years I spent about three months out of each year fulfilling that apostolic mandate. The Lord confirmed what I was doing many times with some amazing miracles.

The first time I landed in India was on my way to Singapore. I only spent two hours there while our plane took on more passengers. The Lord led me to do some praying as I sat on the plane. I saw major strongholds being torn down as I prayed. We then took off and flew to Singapore and then on to Australia. When I returned home there was a letter on my desk from an Indian pastor who had read one of my books in New York! He must have been reading it at almost the same time that I was praying for his country. He invited me to go to India and I later went and saw many miracles. Also, the same week that I got back an Indian lady walked into our church and said that she had been to many churches in our city but nobody was able to lead her to Christ. She got saved and later most of her family came to Christ. That was the first time that we had ever seen a Hindu come into our church! That helped me to realise just how powerful this kind of apostolic praying really is!

Another thing that has often happened is that once I have been and prayed over a country we have heard of wonderful breakthroughs in people getting saved in the same place where we have prayed.

Once when I was preaching in Singapore, the Holy Spirit told me to go and pray for Japan. Peter was with me and so after we had finished in Singapore we flew into Tokyo just for thirty-six hours to pray over Japan. We went right into the heart of Tokyo and up the Tokyo tower where we did some major warfare. I really did not enjoy my time in Japan and said to the Lord that I never wanted to go there again.

The years passed and I never went back to Japan. Then, in 2002 the Holy Spirit spoke to me and said that I was going to Japan soon. My heart sank but I said that I would obey whatever God said to me. Anyway, during the 2002 Dallas ICA conference apostle Ron Sawka from Japan came up to me and invited me to go and minister in Japan. I knew straight away that it was from the Lord and so I agreed. I have been three times in just ten months and have had a tremendous time in Japan. God has given me real love for the people out there and I am just preparing for another trip in a few weeks time.

Many years ago I went to Seoul in Korea and prayed for a few days. I am going to preach at two conferences in South Korea in a few weeks time. There is power in prayer!

Another aspect of apostolic praying happens when we are ministering to people. I was invited to a large church in Chicago one time and the apostle and his wife were standing about fifteen feet away from me. It was the end of a busy weekend of ministry and I felt led to pray for him and his wife. As I did, the power of God knocked them both to the floor and they began shaking for about ten minutes. They could not get off the floor for quite some time. Finally, he sat up still semi-overcome by the Holy Spirit and told the people that they were now going to take up an offering for the visiting speaker. Not only were the people shocked but I was too! This was shortly after my visit from Jesus Christ.

'Praying always with all prayer and supplication in the Spirit, and watching thereunto with all perseverance and supplication for all saints.' (Ephesians 6:18)

*'Confess your faults one to another, and pray one for another, that ye may be healed. **The effectual fervent prayer of a righteous man availeth much.**'*
(James 5:16, emphasis added)

Chapter 14

Apostolic Impartation

Take a look at the following scriptures:

> 'For I long to see you, **that I may impart unto you some spiritual gift**, to the end ye may be established.'
>
> (Romans 1:11, emphasis added)

> 'Neglect not the gift that is in thee, which was given thee by prophecy, with the laying on of the hands of the presbytery.'
>
> (1 Timothy 4:14)

> 'As every man hath received the gift, even so minister the same one to another, as good stewards of the manifold grace of God.'
>
> (1 Peter 4:10)

One of the functions of an apostle is to impart the nine spiritual gifts to establish the Body of Christ. Hence the need for travelling and speaking to different congregations.

I had been used by God in the operation of the spiritual gifts for about ten years when the Holy Spirit said to me, 'Now that you are established in these gifts I will now bring people to you and you will impart them to those I lead you to.' I then discovered these verses in that context and sure enough people started to come to me and ask for me to impart these gifts to them. I did this individually for several years and then the Lord moved me on to impart publicly often in huge meetings. These gifts are mentioned by Paul in the following passage:

> *'For to one is given by the Spirit the word of wisdom; to another the word of knowledge by the same Spirit;*
> *To another faith by the same Spirit; to another the gifts of healing by the same Spirit;*
> *To another the working of miracles; to another prophecy; to another discerning of spirits; to another divers kinds of tongues; to another the interpretation of tongues:*
> *But all these worketh that one and the selfsame Spirit, dividing to every man severally as he will.'*
>
> (1 Corinthians 12:8–11)

The Lord had equipped me with all nine of these over a period of about eight years of pastoral ministry. I had asked for and coveted these precious gifts to help people to bring healing, deliverance and direction to their lives. These gifts are not to build your ministry but to help people at their point of need.

I am often asked to speak at leaders' meetings where the five-fold ministry gifts are present and the Lord will often move upon me to impart both individually and corporately. I have often witnessed angels laying their hands on those that I have prayed for.

Apostolic impartation is so important to equip the Body of Christ and establish the people to do the works of ministry themselves after we have gone.

What is the point in us simply demonstrating the Kingdom with signs and wonders and then leaving them with nothing? This is such a needy aspect of apostolic ministry and I pray that many more get a revelation of it.

This leads us to another aspect of apostolic ministry. That is of recognising other five-fold giftings and helping to release them. In my travels I have often seen senior pastors going through the same struggle that I had over accepting the apostolic mantle. I have been able to confirm both to the leader and his church that this is the correct way to go. That is often all that is needed for someone to take up the baton and start running with it!

This includes ordination, of course, which is definitely apostolic!

> *'For this cause left I thee in Crete, that thou shouldest set in order the things that are wanting, and ordain elders in every city, as I had appointed thee.'*   (Titus 1:5)

> *'And when they had ordained them elders in every church, and had prayed with fasting, they commended them to the Lord, on whom they believed.'*   (Acts 14:23)

> *'Whereunto I am ordained a preacher, and an apostle, (I speak the truth in Christ, and lie not;) a teacher of the Gentiles in faith and verity.'*   (1 Timothy 2:7)

We have an ordination programme which includes three exams that those interested have to complete. Then a person has to prove their calling to my satisfaction and then I will ordain them, which I have done many times now.

Chapter 15

The Day I Had to
Hand Over the Church

The Lord had called upon me to pioneer the mother church of Life Changing Ministries. I had always loved pastoring, having come into full-time ministry very early in life at just twenty-one years of age. Therefore, pastoring and developing people had been my main thrust for a long time. However, I always knew that one day I would hand over the church to my wife since God had shown that to me years before. We were ministering as a team for many years, as I would be in charge of the church when I was at home, and would hand over the reins when I would travel away to minister. Then when I returned I would take full charge of the church, much to Ruth's relief, and she would assist me along with the other faithful ministers that we have.

Thus, I was functioning as a pastor when I was at home and an apostle when I travelled. Now, for many in this situation, it can stay like that. Some apostles are primarily pastors of strong local churches who have great influence in their own territory. Others do a split between pastoring and travelling. Anyway, I had already spoken to Ruth about handing over completely to her as pastor and I would be her apostle. However, every time I asked her if she felt ready to take over she would say no. I was patient since I could see her confidence in ministry growing all of the time and did not want to force her into something before she was ready. Then one day I had a meeting with Ruth and asked her if she was ready because I knew that something was happening to me regarding the pastoral ministry. She said no she was not ready and so I asked her if she would ever be ready! She said no! I knew at that point that I had to make the decision to hand over and take the step of faith of going into full-time apostolic ministry. The well was drying up in me for pastoring and had virtually died inside me, whereas the fire for the apostolic was getting stronger and more intense. So we decided a date and I told the church that I was handing over the pastorship of the church to Ruth with me still being in overall charge. As I did that and laid my hands on Ruth I saw into the spirit realm and I watched Jesus lay His hands on her after I had. At that point I was very confident that I made the right decision.

During the months prior to me handing over I had noticed a major change taking place in me. I could tell that the gift of pastor was drying up rapidly and I was starting to hurt people because of it! We had a few folk leave during our transition, mostly due to this process.

It was a tremendous step of faith for me in so many ways since I did not know where all of my speaking appointments would come from or the finances. I knew that I could visit the churches in our network but I needed far more invitations than that. As the months went by the Lord provided for us as He always had, but we were in new territory now. Also, the Lord had told me to take the step of faith to fly business class on all international flights which meant another £10,000 ($19,000) a year to find. That was over three years ago and I can testify that God is faithful. My offerings have quadrupled to provide for business travel and everywhere I go my offerings keep increasing. I have just had my first six figure offering in pounds! Hallelujah! It pays to obey the Lord. Also, I have just taken the step of faith to fly first class on all international flights. That is another £20,000 ($38,000) a year to find.

I can honestly say that our ministry has developed very much since I took that step. The church is also doing well with Ruth as pastor. We have had many more churches that have joined with us over the past three years and can feel God's pleasure in what I am doing. We are also about to launch a weekly TV programme to reach our nation and beyond through the media.

Just take the next step! That is all we have to do!

Chapter 16

Recent Apostles

There have always been apostles throughout Church history who have opened up new territories for the Kingdom of God. God has raised up apostles in different movements and denominations. He has also used apostles to set up whole new branches of the Kingdom of God all over the world.

I once had the privilege of going to Angeles Temple in Los Angeles to see the magnificent building that Aimee Semple Macpherson built during the depression years. God used Aimee to raise up a whole denomination called the Foursquare Church which is going stronger than ever today. Aimee was certainly an apostle who travelled extensively as well as raising up a church that had around 20,000 each Sunday! I know that many people challenge the fact that a woman can be an apostle but they cannot deny Aimee's amazing ministry. My wife is a senior pastor and doing a great job and I know many women who are doing all types of ministry who have a definite call upon their life.

Another recent apostle was John Wimber who started the Vineyard movement. God used John greatly to influence many of the traditional denominations and introduce the supernatural gifts of the Spirit. He also raised up a strong local church in Anaheim, California, as well as spearheading a global network of Vineyard churches. That can only be the work of an apostle. It is beyond the scope of the other four ministry gifts.

In the UK there are several apostles who have made a real

impact on different branches of the Church of Jesus Christ. Wynne Lewis went to Kensington Temple when there were only about 200 members. He took it to 7,000 members in just seven years with over 100 nationalities. Others include Gerald Coates of Pioneer, Bryn Jones of Harvestime, Terry Virgo of New Frontiers and Colin Urquhart of Kingdom Faith. All of these have established strong local churches as well as birthed other churches throughout Britain and beyond.

Smith Wigglesworth was a man who is talked about all over the world in just about every part of the Kingdom for his faith and outstanding miracles. He was called the 'apostle of faith' who was used by God to raise at least eighteen people from the dead. There were also two brothers called George and Stephen Jeffreys who both established a movement, called Elim and Assemblies of God, respectively. They had a third brother called Edward who also started a small group of churches. What an anointing upon one family! These were all apostles but may not have either realised or accepted such an office.

I believe that the Lord is speaking to many people around the world about their role as an apostle – locally, nationally or even internationally. Once you accept this calling you don't know where it might lead! I never imagined that I would preach in sixty countries!

I like what Paul says about how he received his apostolic mantle:

> **'Paul, an apostle, (not of men, neither by man, but by Jesus Christ, and God the Father,** *who raised him from the dead;)* ...
>
> *But I certify you, brethren, that the gospel which was preached of me is not after man.*
>
> **For I neither received it of man, neither was I taught it, but by the revelation of Jesus Christ.'**
>
> (Galatians 1:1, 11–12, emphasis added)

Other ministries can confirm the call upon your life but I believe that a person knows when he is an apostle. God spoke directly to me about it and it was my responsibility to act on it when the time was right.

My advice to anyone who is unsure about this whole area is to be patient regarding the apostolic and not to be influenced by others if you have heard from heaven yourself. It is one thing to be told by a prophet that you are an apostle but has Jesus told you Himself? You must have the primary word from heaven and not just the secondary word from men on earth.

I pray that more and more apostles rise up and take their place, which will have a domino effect on releasing others into their calling to the glory of God.

Chapter 17

Apostolic Miracles

'And God wrought special miracles by the hands of Paul,
So that from his body were brought unto the sick hand-
kerchiefs or aprons, and the diseases departed from them,
and the evil spirits went out of them.'   (Acts 19:11–12)

The word 'special' in verse 11 above literally means; 'special special special'.

Thus apostles are to demonstrate and experience the most outstanding miracles to impact situations and to see supernatural increase.

I went to a church in Texas on my first visit by invitation of an apostle. His son was the pastor of the church at that time. All afternoon I was battling with a very unusual word from the Lord. I felt that God was telling me to rebuke the pastor publicly in front of the whole church! I had never done anything like before. It was such a strong impression that I could not ignore it. I was invited up to the pulpit after the praise and worship time and the apostle who had invited me was sitting and watching! I went straight for it by saying to the pastor, 'I have a word for you from the Lord.' He got excited and looked up at me very hungry to hear what God was going to say to him. I said this to him: 'The Lord wants to rebuke you publicly over these three areas of your life that you have neglected.' As I said those words he just fell onto the floor with his face to the floor. I then gave the church a

good telling off and told them to repent. I then gave an
appeal for salvation and four people accepted Jesus. I then
preached and ministered healing etc. The pastor then took
me for a meal and told me what had been happening. He
said that God had told him to repent of those three things
that I had named that night. If he did not repent then God
would send a prophet who would publicly rebuke him in
front of the church! I was the man. From that word the
church grew from 160 members to 500 members in just
twelve months. I think the pastor repented! That would be
called an apostolic prophetic rebuke.

I was taking a team of about six from our ministry out to
Sri Lanka and India to speak at various places and one of our
pastors asked me if I would go up to Kathmandu on that trip
also and help the church in Nepal. It was a busy trip as it was
but I agreed to go. A small group of churches decided to join
Life Changing Ministries and the Lord has done some
wonderful things since in that nation. It has grown so much
so that we now have a church in every town in the country
along with an orphanage and full-time Christian school.
The apostolic anointing has helped to establish the church
and it has literally multiplied from a few hundred to over
6,000 people. Many signs and wonders have taken place
there also and Philip and Margaret Evans go out each year to
teach the pastors and to establish them in the things of God.

Another remarkable thing that happens is in the area of
financial giving. Many have sown seed into my ministry and
seen one hundred fold returns very quickly. I was recently in
Japan and a couple sowed $1,000 into my ministry. Within a
few weeks they were given $100,000 which is exactly 100
times what they sowed. Also, in Osaka, many people sowed a
seed for a new car and within a few months 25% had had
their new car! Glory to God. They are certainly seeing the
prophets' reward!

One time I received a letter from a precious pastor in Sri

Lanka asking if I would go and visit. He had fasted for three days after reading one of my books. I felt it was the will of God to go and so I took a team with me to Gampola, Sri Lanka. There were only about forty people when we first went but by the second visit the church had grown to 120 plus four other churches! Now that is apostolic growth!

I have also seen hundreds of personal miracles of healing, deliverance and other miracles. I recently prayed for a guy in a healing line just for general healing. A few weeks later I was handed a letter saying that during that healing line I prayed for a man who had never been able to write at all even in childhood. He was in his fifties and after I had prayed for him he could write for the first time in his life. He could only express himself in pictures before that! I was awed by such a miracle.

I was in Australia a few years ago and the apostle of a large church asked me to speak for him. I had preached for him the previous year and I had noticed that he was very over-weight and that his knees had bowed out. However, when I saw him this next year he was so thin! He had gone on a very strict fast of just fruit each morning five days a week and then eat normally at the weekend for a whole year! He had lost a lot of weight. However, his knees were still bowed and giving him a lot of pain. On the Sunday evening I gave an appeal for healing and miracles and he was the first out to be prayed for. I prayed a simple prayer of healing and I could tell that he had received as I heard him thanking God for his healing. I was due to speak at their healing service on the following Wednesday but I would not be seeing the apostle until then. I did not think much about it and simply went to the healing service all prepared on the Wednesday. The apostle got up and told the congregation what had happened since Sunday night. He said that on the Monday he expected to get up and jump out of bed but he said that the pain had got worse. By the Monday night he was still in much pain. On the Tuesday morning he tried to get up but it worse still and the pain was really bad. At this point I nearly walked out as this testimony was not going to produce much faith in those being prayed for! The apostle then said that he kept in faith and kept praising God for the healing. He then said that by the Tuesday evening not only was all the pain gone but his legs were now straight as before! He was jumping around and dancing for joy! There was an uproar of praise and the faith of the people was sky high. Hallelujah!

I have always had a quest to see mighty miracles to help people and over the years there has been a slow increase in manifestations and I pray that it continues to grow for the glory of God.

> *'Believest thou not that I am in the Father, and the Father in me? The words that I speak unto you I speak not of myself: but the Father that dwelleth in me, he doeth the works.*
>
> *Believe me that I am in the Father, and the Father in me: or else believe me for the very works' sake.*
>
> *Verily, verily, I say unto you,* **He that believeth on me, the works that I do shall he do also; and greater works than these shall he do; because I go unto my Father.**
>
> **And whatsoever ye shall ask in my name, that will I do, that the Father may be glorified in the Son.**
>
> **If ye shall ask any thing in my name, I will do it.**'
>
> (John 14:10–14, emphasis added)

Chapter 18

The First Apostles

'And it came to pass in those days, that he went out into a mountain to pray, and continued all night in prayer to God.

And when it was day, he called unto him his disciples: and of them he chose twelve, whom also he named apostles;

Simon, (whom he also named Peter,) and Andrew his brother, James and John, Philip and Bartholomew,

Matthew and Thomas, James the son of Alphaeus, and Simon called Zelotes,

And Judas the brother of James, and Judas Iscariot, which also was the traitor.'   (Luke 6:12–16)

These early apostles who were first chosen by Jesus were in a completely unique time since they could see Jesus face to face, hear Him talk, and even touch Him.

As the Apostle John recounts:

'That which was from the beginning, which we have heard, which we have seen with our eyes, which we have looked upon, and our hands have handled, of the Word of life;

(For the life was manifested, and we have seen it, and bear witness, and shew unto you that eternal life, which was with the Father, and was manifested unto us;)

That which we have seen and heard declare we unto you, that ye also may have fellowship with us: and truly

> *our fellowship is with the Father, and with his Son Jesus*
> *Christ.'*   (1 John 1:1–3)

Only the initial apostles could say what John is saying here as they were actually with him in the flesh.

Now, this brings us to a very interesting subject. These apostles had no opportunity to walk by faith! They could only ever experience sense knowledge since they could see Jesus Christ.

I love the account when Jesus confronts Thomas over his unbelief:

> *'But Thomas, one of the twelve, called Didymus, was not with them when Jesus came.*
>
> *The other disciples therefore said unto him, We have seen the Lord. But he said unto them, Except I shall see in his hands the print of the nails, and put my finger into the print of the nails, and thrust my hand into his side, I will not believe.*
>
> *And after eight days again his disciples were within, and Thomas with them: then came Jesus, the doors being shut, and stood in the midst, and said, Peace be unto you.*
>
> *Then saith he to Thomas, Reach hither thy finger, and behold my hands; and reach hither thy hand, and thrust it into my side: and be not faithless, but believing.*
>
> *And Thomas answered and said unto him, My Lord and my God.*
>
> ***Jesus saith unto him, Thomas, because thou hast seen me, thou hast believed: blessed are they that have not seen, and yet have believed.'***
>
> (John 20:24–29, emphasis added)

That is one of the reasons why we can do greater works than the early apostles because we walk by faith. It is interesting to note what happened to them all when Jesus was taken captive.

'And Jesus saith unto them, All ye shall be offended because of me this night: for it is written, I will smite the shepherd, and the sheep shall be scattered.

But after that I am risen, I will go before you into Galilee.

But Peter said unto him, Although all shall be offended, yet will not I.

And Jesus saith unto him, Verily I say unto thee, That this day, even in this night, before the cock crow twice, thou shalt deny me thrice.

But he spake the more vehemently, If I should die with thee, I will not deny thee in any wise. Likewise also said they all.' (Mark 14:27–31)

This is all because of walking by sight and not by faith! However, this is how the Lord had ordained it since one of the qualifications of the first apostles was to have seen Jesus in the flesh and be a witness of the resurrection.

'For it is written in the book of Psalms, Let his habitation be desolate, and let no man dwell therein: and his bishoprick let another take.

Wherefore of these men which have companied with us all the time that the Lord Jesus went in and out among us,

Beginning from the baptism of John, unto that same day that he was taken up from us, must one be ordained to be a witness with us of his resurrection.

And they appointed two, Joseph called Barsabas, who was surnamed Justus, and Matthias. (Acts 1:20–23)

As we know Matthias took Judas Iscariot's place.

Even though these men were walking by sight and had denied Him, Jesus still used them mightily! After they had been filled with the Holy Spirit they became fearless for the gospel and obviously gained a great deal of faith to do the things that they accomplished in the Acts of the Apostles.

You will notice though that it is Paul the apostle who has given us the vast majority of teaching on faith, since he was not around at the time of Jesus in the flesh. Therefore he had to walk by faith. Maybe that is why he wrote two thirds of the New Testament!

> *'For therein is the righteousness of God revealed from faith to faith: as it is written, **The just shall live by faith.**'*
> (Romans 1:17, emphasis added)

> *'**Now the just shall live by faith: but if any man draw back, my soul shall have no pleasure in him.**'*
> (Hebrews 10:38, emphasis added)

> *'Now faith is the substance of things hoped for, the evidence of things not seen.'* (Hebrews 11:1)

> *'**But without faith it is impossible to please him:** for he that cometh to God must believe that he is, and that he is a rewarder of them that diligently seek him.'*
> (Hebrews 11:6, emphasis added)

We must walk by faith in order to please God. This is absolutely paramount in the apostolic ministry and must surely go with the territory. Your faith must be high all the time in order to fulfil any apostolic venture. I can now understand why my faith has been tested and tried so many times over the last twenty-five years! It has all been in preparation for the apostolic.

Chapter 19

Apostolic Deliverance

When I first entered Christian ministry the first question that I asked my pastor was, 'What would I do if I met somebody who needed deliverance from demons?'

Aubrey smiled with his trademark broad smile and sat me down and taught me for ten weeks about casting out devils. I was absolutely amazed at some of his stories as he encountered demonic situations. He gave me a lot of teaching from the Word of God and dozens of examples during his pastoral duties. He also explained the operation of the gift of discerning of spirits to me and as he did that particular gift began to work through me. Aubrey told me that it was a dull ache in the palm of his left hand almost like a spike going through the centre of the hand. He said that every time that anointing came upon him he knew that he would have to cast out demons within twenty-four hours. That was nearly twenty-five years ago and in all of those years the same thing has happened to me on hundreds of occasions. That anointing would come in to my left hand and within a short time I would have to minister to someone who needed to be set free from a demon either in person or over the telephone. Nowadays this anointing, along with others, usually come upon me as I get onto a plane to go and minister in another country in preparation for signs and wonders.

In the early days of ministry I would only minister to one individual at a time for deliverance. However, the Lord has taught me so much over the years about the corporate anointing for deliverance which saves so much time and energy on my part. I can now minister to hundreds and even thousands at a time just by speaking out from the front. Some cases, however, still need the personal touch particularly when ministering to leaders.

I believe that deliverance ministry is a major part of the ministry of an apostle. Paul had a deliverance ministry along with Jesus, of course. As I have travelled around I have often been called upon to minister deliverance to senior leaders behind the scenes. This has happened numerous times all over the world. If apostles don't minister deliverance to leaders who need it then who will?

I have written a major book on this ministry called *Angels, Demons and Spiritual Warfare*, which has been my best-selling book now for over eight years.

As the years have passed and I have had to deal with different cases, I have realised that deliverance is needed in so many different areas:

1. The mind.
2. The emotions.
3. The intellect.
4. Hereditary.
5. Flash backs to bad experiences.
6. The personality.
7. The sexual area.
8. The occult.
9. Upbringing.
10. Religious spirits.
11. Victims of control.
12. Spirits of infirmity.

These twelve cover the vast majority of cases.

I learnt so much about number 6 – the area of personality – by ministering to my own wife many years ago. She was so quiet, shy and reserved and we both thought that that was how she was born and would never change.

We had a real move of deliverance in our church many years ago, and one day Ruth came to me and asked me if I thought she needed deliverance. I said, 'I don't think so but I will pray for you anyway.' As I prayed she began manifesting all sorts of things and so I ministered to her over a three-year period in all aspects of her being. The most amazing thing that I learned was that Ruth's personality was so bound by the demonic it caused her to be shy, have a crushed spirit, feel inferior, insecure etc. After she was set free she told me that she always knew that the real Ruth was locked inside and whenever she tried to express herself it would come out all wrong. Therefore she had become very insular and frustrated. However, as she received deliverance, her whole personality changed and she is now a senior pastor. She is not the same person that I married as she has changed beyond all recognition. She has a good self-image now, confident, bold and able to express herself in most situations.

Since I ministered to Ruth I have met so many people like her who need this kind of freedom. The problem is that many who minister deliverance do not include personality deliverance in their repertoire. I have thus had the joy of setting people free in their personality as well as more obvious areas.

> 'Heal the sick, cleanse the lepers, raise the dead, cast out devils: freely ye have received, freely give.'   (Matthew 10:8)

> 'But if I cast out devils by the Spirit of God, then the kingdom of God is come unto you.'   (Matthew 12:28)

> 'And he preached in their synagogues throughout all Galilee, and cast out devils.'   (Mark 1:39)

> *'And he ordained twelve, that they should be with him, and that he might send them forth to preach,*
>
> *And to have power to heal sicknesses, and to cast out devils.'*   (Mark 3:14–15)

> *'And these signs shall follow them that believe; In my name shall they cast out devils; they shall speak with new tongues.'*
>
> (Mark 16:17)

> *'The same day there came certain of the Pharisees, saying unto him, Get thee out, and depart hence: for Herod will kill thee.*
>
> *And he said unto them, Go ye, and tell that fox, Behold, I cast out devils, and I do cures to day and to morrow, and the third day I shall be perfected.'*   (Luke 13:31–32)

Here we see the initial twelve given the mandate the cast out demons even before they were even born again or filled with the Holy Spirit! How much more should we be casting out devils!

Casting out devils is a demonstration of the Kingdom of God.

Some say that you should not go looking for demons. I agree! I don't need to go looking for them as there are plenty of them about and particularly in the Church of Jesus Christ! Many times they come looking for me!

There is also a close link between many sicknesses and demonic activity. Many times when I am asked to pray for somebody regarding sickness or disease in their body I will start to pray and they will begin to manifest and so I simply cast out the spirit and the person gets healed. Also, some diseases and ailments are hereditary and you have to set them free from ancestral curses. I have done this many times and seen folk get healed. Sometimes deliverance is part of the healing process and other things such as forgiveness need to be addressed.

If you have never been used in this ministry of deliverance then why not ask the Lord to help you. Ask Him if you need any deliverance yourself and begin by setting yourself free! Every born again Spirit-filled believer who speaks in tongues has the authority to drive out demons. It should be the most natural thing. I have noticed over the last few years that more and more people are talking about this ministry and indeed doing it! Praise God. This is part of the end-time restoration of all that has been stolen.

Chapter 20

Apostolic Finances

I have always known that God would provide for me since He is Jehovah Jireh, the God who provides. Paul also says:

> *'But my God shall supply all your need according to his riches in glory by Christ Jesus.'* (Philippians 4:19)

When Ruth and I were first married we did not have much revelation of biblical finances. All we knew was that God would look after us. We went from one miracle to another with money coming through the post, food parcels on the doorstep etc. Each time we rejoiced and did not know any other way. We had not been taught about God's system of finances, about sowing specific seeds. All we knew was that we were to tithe and God would open the windows of heaven. Our need always got met but that was all that we were believing for! You only get what you are believing for!

Over the years our understanding has grown and developed and I am now going to show you how we generate finances in every aspect of our lives both in our personal life and ministry.

Tithing comes first into the local church, which is the storehouse:

> *'Will a man rob God? Yet ye have robbed me. But ye say, Wherein have we robbed thee? In tithes and offerings.*

Ye are cursed with a curse: for ye have robbed me, even this whole nation.

Bring ye all the tithes into the storehouse, that there may be meat in mine house, and prove me now herewith, saith the Lord *of hosts, if I will not open you the windows of heaven, and pour you out a blessing, that there shall not be room enough to receive it.*

And I will rebuke the devourer for your sakes, and he shall not destroy the fruits of your ground; neither shall your vine cast her fruit before the time in the field, saith the Lord *of hosts.*

And all nations shall call you blessed: for ye shall be a delightsome land, saith the Lord *of hosts.'*

(Malachi 3:8–12)

That is fundamental. The Word of God says that the tithe is holy and belongs to the Lord.

However, something that I missed for many years was the seed above the tithe.

The law of Genesis is that everything reproduces after its own kind.

'And God said, Let the earth bring forth grass, the herb yielding seed, and the fruit tree yielding fruit after his kind, whose seed is in itself, upon the earth: and it was so.

And the earth brought forth grass, and herb yielding seed after his kind, and the tree yielding fruit, whose seed was in itself, after his kind: and God saw that it was good.'

(Genesis 1:11–12)

So does money. Look at these scriptures:

*'But this I say, **He which soweth sparingly shall reap also sparingly; and he which soweth bountifully shall reap also bountifully**.*

*Every man according as he purposeth in his heart, so
let him give; not grudgingly, or of necessity: for God loveth a
cheerful giver.*

*And God is able to make all grace abound toward you; that
ye, always having all sufficiency in all things, may abound to
every good work:*

*(As it is written, He hath dispersed abroad; he hath given
to the poor: his righteousness remaineth for ever.*

*Now he that ministereth seed to the sower both minister
bread for your food, and* **multiply your seed sown,** *and
increase the fruits of your righteousness;)*

*Being enriched in every thing to all bountifulness, which
causeth through us thanksgiving to God.'*

(2 Corinthians 9:6–11, emphasis added)

Also the principle of multiplication is mentioned by Jesus
Himself:

*'But he shall receive an hundredfold now in this time, houses,
and brethren, and sisters, and mothers, and children, and
lands, with persecutions; and in the world to come eternal
life.'*   (Mark 10:30)

*'A sower went out to sow his seed: and as he sowed, some fell
by the way side; and it was trodden down, and the fowls of
the air devoured it.*

*And some fell upon a rock; and as soon as it was sprung
up, it withered away, because it lacked moisture.*

*And some fell among thorns; and the thorns sprang up
with it, and choked it.*

*And other fell on good ground, and sprang up, and bare
fruit an hundredfold. And when he had said these things,
he cried, He that hath ears to hear, let him hear.'*

(Luke 8:5–8)

As well as in the Old Testament:

> **'Then Isaac sowed in that land, and received in the
> same year an hundredfold: and the LORD blessed him.'**
> (Genesis 26:12, emphasis added)

Thus the hundredfold principle has been in operation for thousands of years!

In practice this is what Ruth and I do. We plan ahead in our finances often for a year at a time and we sow specific seeds to generate money for different projects. For instance at the start of 2004 the trustees of LCM sowed many seeds for books to be published, equipment, outreach etc. We named each seed and confessed for a one hundred fold return on each seed. This is above our tithe which we give into other ministries. Within a few short months all of our seeds had harvested and we were able to purchase all sorts of things for the ministry.

I am always needing money for flights as I am overseas for about sixteen weeks out of every year. In January I sowed five seeds for my next five trips to generate £15,000 ($29,000) for the first six months ministry. I sowed just one percent which was £150 ($290) and named my seed specifically. It took just six weeks for the money to come in. We do that for cars, holidays, book publishing, fridges, houses etc. It works for everything! It's so simple. The other thing about money is making a strict debt free rule! You will only ever experience partial prosperity if you borrow money and I will show you why. Take a look at the following scriptures:

> *'The LORD shall open unto thee his good treasure, the heaven
> to give the rain unto thy land in his season, and to bless all
> the work of thine hand: and **thou shalt lend unto many
> nations, and thou shalt not borrow.***

> ***And the*** L***ORD*** ***shall make thee the head, and not the tail; and thou shalt be above only, and thou shalt not be beneath;*** *if that thou hearken unto the commandments of the* L*ORD* *thy God, which I command thee this day, to observe and to do them.'*
> (Deuteronomy 28:12–13, emphasis added)

> *'The rich ruleth over the poor, and* ***the borrower is servant to the lender.'***   (Proverbs 22:7, emphasis added)

> ***'Owe no man any thing, but to love one another:*** *for he that loveth another hath fulfilled the law.*
> (Romans 13:8, emphasis added)

Thus, if you borrow you become the tail instead of the head. God does not want that at all! We are supposed to be kings and priests, ambassadors of the New Testament!

Also we are servants of the most High God and not a borrowing institute!

Then Paul gives us a command! I think that *'Owe no man any thing'* is clear enough!

Ruth and I made that decision about twelve years ago to get out of debt. We had borrowed for a car and it got us into trouble. I was also using a credit card and had built up quite a debt. We repented and sowed specific seeds to clear our debts. It took about eighteen months to clear them all but it felt so good when we were free of all debt at last.

You will never know what it is like until you make a quality decision to live debt free. I know you are probably thinking that you are doing alright now but just think how prosperous you could become if you get in line with God's Word and get out of debt! I challenge you to do it. You will never look back.

Many ask me the obvious question, 'What about a mortgage?' Good question. May I ask you a question? Is a

mortgage a debt? What happens if you stop making pay-
ments? A mortgage is just as much a debt as any other. Is
there a better way? I am going to tell you what we are doing
and you can make your own mind up.

Firstly, is it the will of God to own your own house? I
believe that it is most certainly His will.

> *'Lest when thou hast eaten and art full, and hast built goodly
> houses, and dwelt therein.'* (Deuteronomy 8:12)

> *'Wealth and riches shall be in his house: and his right-
> eousness endureth for ever.'* (Psalm 112:3)

> *'House and riches are the inheritance of fathers and a
> prudent wife is from the Lord.'* (Proverbs 19:14)

Thus it is definitely God's will for us to have nice house.

Anyway about eleven years ago Ruth and I began to sow
specific seeds for a house. Each month we would sow and
name a seed above our tithe just for a house. We worked out
approximately how much our dream house would cost and
knew that we needed to sow a one percent seed. It took us
three years sowing each month to sow enough for the house
that we wanted. We have added to those seeds over the years
just to make sure! Also, we have added to the kind of house
that we would like! Hallelujah!

In the meantime we have rented our home which Paul did
in the book of Acts:

> *'And Paul dwelt two whole years in his own hired
> house, and received all that came in unto him.'*
> (Acts 28:30, emphasis added)

In the first few years we saw no harvest at all. We kept
believing and confessing God's Word over our seed. You

need a consistent confession of faith or else you will dig up your seed.

In the last few years we have seen some amazing harvests towards our house. We have about 70% at the time of writing in capital to pay cash for our own home. We have done it with cars and always pay cash for our cars. I have just paid cash for an S-type Jaguar V8 which is definitely apostolic! I also paid cash for Ruth's car using the same principles. It keeps you debt free. All you need is to sow specific seeds into debt free soil and wait patiently for the harvest.

> *'That ye be not slothful, but followers of them who through faith and patience inherit the promises.'*   (Hebrews 6:12)

> *'And so, after he had patiently endured, he obtained the promise.'*   (Hebrews 6:15)

> *'Knowing this, that the trying of your faith worketh patience.'*
>   (James 1:3)

> *'Be not deceived; God is not mocked: for whatsoever a man soweth, that shall he also reap.*
>   *For he that soweth to his flesh shall of the flesh reap corruption; but he that soweth to the Spirit shall of the Spirit reap life everlasting.*
>   *And let us not be weary in well doing: for in due season we shall reap, if we faint not.'*   (Galatians 6:7–9)

This is now life-style for us and it works quicker now than ever. Think about it!

Chapter 21

The Holy Spirit and Finances

If any ministry needs to be listening to the Holy Spirit then apostles certainly do! I have had a quest in my life to listen to His voice on a daily basis and I spend quality time in fellowship with the Lord to make myself available to Him whenever He wants to speak to me about anything. This has been a developing relationship over the last twenty-five years. The Scriptures do say:

> *'My sheep hear my voice, and I know them, and they follow me'* (John 10:27, emphasis added)

> *'He that hath an ear, let him hear what the Spirit saith unto the churches;* To him that overcometh will I give to eat of the tree of life, which is in the midst of the paradise of God.' (Revelation 2:7, emphasis added)

> *'Howbeit when he, the Spirit of truth, is come, he will guide you into all truth:* for he shall not speak of himself; but whatsoever he shall hear, that shall he speak: *and he will shew you things to come.'*
> (John 16:13, emphasis added)

But the Word also says:

> *'Behold, in this thou art not just: I will answer thee, that God is greater than man.*

> *Why dost thou strive against him? for he giveth not account of any of his matters.*
>
> **For God speaketh once, yea twice, yet man perceiveth it not.**
>
> *In a dream, in a vision of the night, when deep sleep falleth upon men, in slumberings upon the bed;*
>
> **Then he openeth the ears of men, and sealeth their instruction,**
>
> **That he may withdraw man from his purpose, and hide pride from man.'**
>
> (Job 33:12–17, emphasis added)

Some people, including preachers, are too busy to hear from God and so they fulfil their own purpose in ministry. Our job is to get our hearts into the place where we can hear God's voice in any situation and for any purpose. I need to hear from the Lord about all sorts of issues. Jesus said:

> *'Abide in me, and I in you. As the branch cannot bear fruit of itself, except it abide in the vine; no more can ye, except ye abide in me.*
>
> *I am the vine, ye are the branches: He that abideth in me, and I in him, the same bringeth forth much fruit: for without me ye can do nothing.*
>
> *If a man abide not in me, he is cast forth as a branch, and is withered; and men gather them, and cast them into the fire, and they are burned.*
>
> *If ye abide in me, and my words abide in you, ye shall ask what ye will, and it shall be done unto you.*
>
> *Herein is my Father glorified, that ye bear much fruit; so shall ye be my disciples.'* (John 15:4–8)

Anything that we do in ministry that is outside of God's will for our lives is going to be burnt up anyway. So our main priority must surely be to listen to His voice and obey all that

He tells us to do. That is what I seek to do all of the time. Jesus never operated independently of the Father. Look at this verse:

> *'And he that sent me is with me: **the Father hath not left me alone; for I do always those things that please him.'***
> (John 8:29, emphasis added)

Jesus was the Son of God and yet He never did anything outside of the will of the Father. How much more should we stay within what He says at all times!

The reason that I am saying all of this is that if you develop this kind of intimacy with Jesus where you are at now and learn to listen to His voice, then when you sail out of the harbour and onto the rough sea you can be confident that He will provide for you.

The Holy Spirit has laid it upon my heart to share something with you about my apostolic travelling that the Lord started with me some years ago in Australia.

I was praying about the money for the trip and can remember asking God for a certain amount of money from my time in Australia, like a faith target. Of course this was private between me and God. I never tell people what I am expecting from any of my trips. That is part of the faith walk. Anyway, I asked the Lord for $4,000 (Australian dollars) and God spoke clearly to me and said that the figure was too low! He then gave me a higher figure of $5,300. It was much more than my previous year but I agreed with the Holy Spirit. I was there for quite a long stint of about twenty-six days. I was preaching all the time and offerings were coming in. On the last day I was at Melbourne airport and I counted the offerings and it was exactly $5,300. You only get what you believe for!

I have since done this everywhere I go and talk to the Lord about the finances before every trip. I don't know what my future outgoings are going to be exactly, but God does! I only have a rough idea. I have recently been to Cornwall in the UK to speak for a few days and before I went I asked the Lord for £2,000. This figure was based on previous visits. However, the Holy Spirit spoke to me and said to ask Him for £3,000. I told nobody and went about speaking, preaching etc. During the last day a precious lady that I had ministered to a few times put in a very large cheque which made up the exact figure of £3,000.

On a recent trip to Japan I was praying about the finances and on the previous trip had received the best offering of my ministry with £19,000 ($37,000). I decided to take a huge step of faith (as I thought) and ask God for £38,000 ($75,000). I released my prayer of faith and the Holy Spirit immediately said to me that the figure was way too small! The Lord then said to me that a lady was going to put an enormous offering into my life on this trip and told me to believe for six figures! I was shocked but did what the Lord has said to me. I preached in Sano and Tokyo and then flew down to Osaka to minister. The offerings were very good as usual, since they ask me to take up my own offerings! It was about £13,000 ($25,000) in total. But no lady. I preached in Osaka and the leaders asked me to take up my own offering which I did. A lady came up to one of the leaders and pledged a huge offering for me of £44,000 ($90,000). They were delighted as they had seen many miracles in the financial realm from my previous trip. However, they wanted me to take up another offering the following day when I spoke. I did and the same lady put in another pledge for £73,000 ($150,000)! She did not put the money in cash for obvious reasons but instead she faithfully sent it through the banking system. What God had shown me was absolutely right and I had my first six figure offering. Hallelujah! That pays me back for the dozens of international trips where Ruth and I have made huge sacrifices for the gospel.

God sees those sacrifices and if we will remain faithful to what He says then He will bless us beyond our wildest dreams.

Therefore, if you are called to travel in ministry then start to sow seed specifically for your trips, listen to the Holy Spirit and see what He says to you!

*'His lord said unto him, Well done, thou good and faithful servant: **thou hast been faithful over a few things, I will make thee ruler over many things:** enter thou into the joy of thy lord.'*   (Matthew 25:21, emphasis added)

Chapter 22

Strict Obedience

I came across a wonderful scripture a few years ago that spoke to me very much.

> **'But this thing commanded I them, saying, Obey my voice, and I will be your God, and ye shall be my people: and walk ye in all the ways that I have commanded you, that it may be well unto you.**
>
> But they hearkened not, nor inclined their ear, but walked in the counsels and in the imagination of their evil heart, **and went backward, and not forward.**
>
> (Jeremiah 7:23–24, emphasis added)

I don't want to go backward at all but want to go forward in each area of my life. What about you?

Every time you obey God it causes you to go forward. But if you then disobey Him it causes you to go backward! Thus, many people find themselves going forward and backward all the time and hence never get anywhere. All we have to do is to obey what He says and God will cause us to bear much fruit! What could be simpler?

That was Saul's problem:

> 'And Samuel said, When thou wast little in thine own sight, wast thou not made the head of the tribes of Israel, and the LORD anointed thee king over Israel?

And the Lord *sent thee on a journey, and said, Go and utterly destroy the sinners the Amalekites, and fight against them until they be consumed.*

Wherefore then didst thou not obey the voice of the Lord, *but didst fly upon the spoil, and didst evil in the sight of the* Lord?

And Saul said unto Samuel, Yea, I have obeyed the voice of the Lord, *and have gone the way which the* Lord *sent me, and have brought Agag the king of Amalek, and have utterly destroyed the Amalekites.*

But the people took of the spoil, sheep and oxen, the chief of the things which should have been utterly destroyed, to sacrifice unto the Lord *thy God in Gilgal.*

And Samuel said, **Hath the** Lord **as great delight in burnt offerings and sacrifices, as in obeying the voice of the** Lord? **Behold, to obey is better than sacrifice, and to hearken than the fat of rams.**

For rebellion is as the sin of witchcraft, and stubbornness is as iniquity and idolatry. *Because thou hast rejected the word of the* Lord, *he hath also rejected thee from being king.*

And Saul said unto Samuel, I have sinned: for I have transgressed the commandment of the Lord, *and thy words: because I feared the people, and obeyed their voice.*

Now therefore, I pray thee, pardon my sin, and turn again with me, that I may worship the Lord.

And Samuel said unto Saul, I will not return with thee: for thou hast rejected the word of the Lord, *and the* Lord *hath rejected thee from being king over Israel.'*

(1 Samuel 15:17–26, emphasis added)

When we are small in our own sight and we make a mistake then nobody gets to hear about it. But when we our sphere of ministry becomes significantly larger then even the smallest thing can be used by the enemy to trip us

up. I believe that if we are obedient in the little things then
the Lord will increase our ministry and we shall see the
kind of fruit that God wants us to see and can entrust us
with.

Look at what Jesus says about obedience:

> '*Herein is my Father glorified, that ye bear much fruit;*
> *so shall ye be my disciples.*
>
> *As the Father hath loved me, so have I loved you: continue*
> *ye in my love.*
>
> *If ye keep my commandments, ye shall abide in my*
> *love; even as I have kept my Father's commandments,*
> *and abide in his love.*
>
> *These things have I spoken unto you, that my joy might*
> *remain in you, and that your joy might be full.*
>
> *This is my commandment, That ye love one another, as I*
> *have loved you.*
>
> *Greater love hath no man than this, that a man lay down*
> *his life for his friends.*
>
> *Ye are my friends, if ye do whatsoever I command*
> *you.*
>
> *Henceforth I call you not servants; for the servant*
> *knoweth not what his lord doeth: but I have called you*
> *friends; for all things that I have heard of my Father I*
> *have made known unto you.*
>
> *Ye have not chosen me, but I have chosen you, and*
> *ordained you, that ye should go and bring forth fruit,*
> *and that your fruit should remain: that whatsoever ye*
> *shall ask of the Father in my name, he may give it you.*'
>
> (John 15:8–16, emphasis added)

If we want to be a friend of Jesus we must do what He says!
Abraham became the friend of God through the same
process:

*'And the scripture was fulfilled which saith, Abraham believed God, and it was imputed unto him for righteousness: and **he was called the Friend of God**.'*

(James 2:23, emphasis added)

All through obedience. It may have taken Abraham a long time to come into line with strict obedience but come into line he did! I love what God said to him after God finally knew that he could trust his servant Abraham in absolutely everything:

'And they came to the place which God had told him of; and Abraham built an altar there, and laid the wood in order, and bound Isaac his son, and laid him on the altar upon the wood.

And Abraham stretched forth his hand, and took the knife to slay his son.

And the angel of the LORD *called unto him out of heaven, and said, Abraham, Abraham: and he said, Here am I.*

*And he said, Lay not thine hand upon the lad, neither do thou any thing unto him: **for now I know that thou fearest God, seeing thou hast not withheld thy son, thine only son from me**.*

And Abraham lifted up his eyes, and looked, and behold behind him a ram caught in a thicket by his horns: and Abraham went and took the ram, and offered him up for a burnt offering in the stead of his son.

And Abraham called the name of that place Jehovah-jireh: as it is said to this day, In the mount of the LORD *it shall be seen.*

And the angel of the LORD *called unto Abraham out of heaven the second time,*

And said, By myself have I sworn, saith the LORD, *for because thou hast done this thing, and hast not withheld thy son, thine only son:*

> *That in blessing I will bless thee, and in multiplying I*
> *will multiply thy seed as the stars of the heaven, and as*
> *the sand which is upon the sea shore; and thy seed*
> *shall possess the gate of his enemies;*
> *And in thy seed shall all the nations of the earth be*
> *blessed; because thou hast obeyed my voice.'*
>
> (Genesis 22:9–18, emphasis added)

As apostles we therefore have an enormous responsibility to those whom we oversee and minister. They need examples to follow of men and women who know their God and obey exactly what He says. The miracles will follow our obedience and they will speak for themselves.

I was preaching in a city in the USA one weekend and I was not enjoying myself. I had a very full schedule and spoke three times on the Sunday in three different churches and then had to fly the next day to speak in another town. The man that I was with took me out for a meal and brought along another guy that he wanted to introduce to me. We sat down to eat and straight away the prophetic word came upon me strongly to speak into this man's life. I told him that he was operating far below his calling and that God was calling him into apostolic ministry. He had been fighting this for a long time and knew that what I was saying was correct. He had been making his age an excuse. But this was the word that God gave to me. 'You have been saying that you are too old to move into an apostolic call but God is saying that it is because of your age that He can trust you to do it!' He thought that he was too old at about fifty-eight years of age. I ended up ministering to him all day at different services since he came to all the places where I was speaking! I really hope that he obeyed the high call upon his life. I have not heard from him but trust that I was able to confirm the word that God had already spoken to him about. He was about twenty years older than me and was also on a ministry team of a very large church. I may have to wait until I get to heaven before I find out!

Just do what God has called you to do. If He has called you to be an apostle then He will confirm it to you as He did with me.

Chapter 23

Workaholism

When I first entered Christian ministry aged twenty-one I was so zealous for the things of God. I worked all the time and enjoyed it so much. However, I did not realise it but I was actually trying to **work for God**! That was my biggest mistake. I wondered why I was always tired. I saw very little fruit for all of my sincere efforts but at least we learned how to live by faith and trust the Lord for everything.

I went from Garston, Liverpool, to another church in Salford. I had not yet realised that I was, in fact, a workaholic! Nobody taught me any differently. Those I saw in ministry were just the same, working all the time and seeing little fruit.

The work was going slowly and one or two were joining us but I knew there was more. I used to make a list of all the people who were not at church on the Sunday and I would visit them all before next Sunday to find out why they had not been at church!

I then went to a conference for leaders and a preacher called John Shelbourne talked about 'working for God'. I said, 'That's me, I'm working for God.' He then went on to say that those of us called into full-time ministry were not supposed to be working for God. It was like a sledgehammer had just hit me. He then gave some scriptures:

'For we are labourers together with God: ye are God's husbandry, ye are God's building.'

(1 Corinthians 3:9, emphasis added)

'We then, as workers together with him, beseech you also that ye receive not the grace of God in vain.'

(2 Corinthians 6:1, emphasis added)

His whole message for just for me. I listened intently as he said that we are supposed to work **with God and not for Him**! I saw it. The revelation came to me. However, I was so used to being a workaholic that it took me six months to stop striving. It was habitual. John went on to say that those who work for God end up having a heart attack or stroke but those who work with God enjoy a life of fulfilment and fruit bearing! What a revelation it was to me. Nobody had ever said those things to me before. Or maybe they had but it had not registered! We are so slow sometimes with such simple truths.

I started to take one day a week just to pray and nothing else and to tune my spirit in with the Holy Spirit.

Amazing things started to happen as the Lord would give me words of instruction to fulfil. 'Go and visit sister thunder muffin.' I would get a series of words of knowledge for Sunday and speak them out and miracles would happen. I began to realise what John was talking about. The more I developed my close personal relationship with God the more fruit I saw in ministry. I was being delivered of workaholism and learning to work **with God and not for Him**. I also noticed that I was experiencing much less stress by simply doing what God showed me to do.

One morning I was having my quiet time and the Lord spoke to me that I had to pray for someone today at a college where I was going to speak. I had been asked to speak on philosophy of religion at a girls' college and so I preached signs and wonders for two hours! I told them how God speaks to me and that miracles happen. They were all ears. Then one of the girls asked me if he had spoken to me about any of them and I said yes! They all got excited. I assumed that I had to pray for one of the girls. However, at the end of the two lessons the girls all went and the teacher was left on her own. She said to me that she was the person that needed to be prayed for. I was quite surprised but I listened to her story. She told me that she was going to commit suicide the night before I was due to be at her lesson but she did not want to cause me any problems and so she was going to kill herself that night! I led her to Christ and she was set free. A few weeks later she was baptised in the Holy Spirit in our lounge and the last I heard about her she was leading people to Jesus and taking them to church with her. It pays to listen and obey! She would have been in hell now if I had not been in tune with the Lord.

Sadly, I have to watch many in ministry working so hard to make things happen and striving all the time. I tell them about working for God and they don't see it! If this is speaking to you about any aspect of service for the Lord then take some time out and make the adjustments necessary. I am seeing so much fruit today compared with all those years ago.

I only do commanded work! Most of the things that I am doing today in ministry I would never have chosen to do. I hated writing at school, I did not want to travel abroad at all! But God has given me a love for the things that I was no good at. This book has only taken me just six days to write! I am up in Scotland just to write this book and it has just poured onto my laptop. No striving at all.

I pray that all those in ministry would learn from my stumbling around and trying to please God by working all the time. Ministry is team work. It is Father and Son working together. Stop working for God ... today!

Chapter 24

The Nature of an Apostle

'For I will not dare to speak of any of those things which Christ hath not wrought by me, to make the Gentiles obedient, by word and deed,
  Through mighty signs and wonders, by the power of the Spirit of God; so that from Jerusalem, and round about unto Illyricum, I have fully preached the gospel of Christ.'
(Romans 15:18–19)

Paul was forever setting out again for some distant land or city to preach the gospel to a new crowd of people.

I have often spoken to pastors and talked to them about travelling out to preach and their response is almost always the same. They usually say that they can't wait to get home to their local church where they pastor. It is somewhat of a burden for them to speak to another congregation.

However, as far as I can remember, I have always had the desire to travel out and minister to a new church or body of people somewhere. That is the essence of the apostolic! An apostle is always looking for a new challenge to his faith, a new mountain top, a higher hurdle to leap over, new territory to break open! A pastor is primarily a maintainer of a flock and longs to see them mature in Christ Jesus. I have pastored four churches in the last twenty years and have enjoyed the challenges that come with looking after the same people but my heart has been to go out and meet

89

new people and turn them on to the Word of God! I enjoy nothing better than to go to a new church or conference and preach to a group of people that I have never met and seek to connect with them as quickly as possible. The Lord has given me a sense of humour for this purpose and laughter is the fastest way to open up a new audience. I don't mean by telling jokes. Some are very good at that and I will leave the joke telling to those who are gifted that way. I seem to be naturally funny for some reason. My wife says that I can get people laughing with no effort at all. I have realised that it must be a gift from God as it certainly opens people up to be able to minister the Word of God to them speedily.

I have often likened the various ministries with a medical doctor. Many doctors begin with general practice but then realise their particular gifting and specialise in one sphere or another. They are actually called specialists!

A pastor is very much a general practitioner who has a wide understanding of people and their needs and is often able to minister to the vast majority of the people.

An apostle is much like a specialist who may have started out as a pastor but then realises where his true anointing is and wants to spend his time just in a few specialist areas. I am very much like that now, particularly as the pastor anointing lifted off me over a season. When I handed the church over to Ruth she was able to fully express herself as a pastor and I was able to move into the fullness of the apostolic calling. At this present time I would find it very difficult to go back into the pastoral ministry as my specialist areas have come even more into focus over the last three years. I know exactly where I function with the highest level of anointing and I also know where I am not anointed.

My main apostolic functions are now overseeing our net-work, writing books, teaching on faith, deliverance, spiritual warfare, prosperity, imparting spiritual gifts, moving in signs and wonders and releasing people into their proper gifting.

It is so important that we know what our calling is. I remember an evangelist once who was in charge of a large church. He was trying to be a pastor when he should have really been on the road concentrating on his most anointed gifting. Instead he began to destroy the church. People began to leave and fortunately he realised what was happening. He stepped down from his pastorate and went out as an itinerant evangelist. There are certain signs that can help us to know that we are in the will of God. Sometimes the will of God changes and we should move on into the next step for our lives. This makes way for the right person to follow us and also enables us to keep fulfilling the high call.

Some of the signs are peace in our heart, fruit that is growing, the proper flow of finances (God pays for what He orders), a content spouse (God can speak through your partner), the advice and counsel of those of our inner circle, but particularly, the Word of God to our own heart! The Lord will show you if you have completed a season of ministry and need to move on if you are listening and not striving. That is why it is good to go away and fast and pray every so often to make sure that all that you are doing is in line with the perfect will of God.

I personally feel that all apostles should have spent many years as a pastor. Having the responsibility for people is so important. Paul was a pastor of three churches that we know about, which is our prototype for the apostolic.

Are you a general practitioner or do you feel more of a specialist? God will make room for your calling as the Word declares:

> *'A man's gift maketh room for him, and bringeth him before great men.'* (Proverbs 18:16)

It should become obvious to those who oversee you as time passes by as to where your gifts are. Sometimes we need patience because the time is not right as yet. His time is always perfect! You may be in a season of preparation for the high calling that God has for you. If He is preparing you then don't run until He says so! Preparation time is vital. Look at how much time the Army has to prepare before it sends its soldiers into battle. You will have to trust the people who have to make such decisions.

> *'For my thoughts are not your thoughts, neither are your ways my ways, saith the* Lord.
>
> *For as the heavens are higher than the earth, so are my ways higher than your ways, and my thoughts than your thoughts.*
>
> *For as the rain cometh down, and the snow from heaven, and returneth not thither, but watereth the earth, and maketh it bring forth and bud, that it may give seed to the sower, and bread to the eater:*
>
> *So shall my word be that goeth forth out of my mouth: it shall not return unto me void, but it shall accomplish that which I please, and it shall prosper in the thing whereto I sent it.*
>
> *For ye shall go out with joy, and be led forth with peace: the mountains and the hills shall break forth before you into singing, and all the trees of the field shall clap their hands.'*
>
> (Isaiah 55:8–12)

Always remember that the five-fold gifts are unique in everyone's life. Also, Jesus Christ is the giver of these gifts and not man.

> *'But unto every one of us is given grace according to the measure of the gift of Christ.*
>
> *Wherefore he saith, When he ascended up on high, he led captivity captive, and gave gifts unto men.*
>
> *(Now that he ascended, what is it but that he also descended first into the lower parts of the earth?*

He that descended is the same also that ascended up far above all heavens, that he might fill all things.)

And he gave some, apostles; and some, prophets; and some, evangelists; and some, pastors and teachers;

For the perfecting of the saints, for the work of the ministry, for the edifying of the body of Christ.'

(Ephesians 4:7–12)

For the gifts and calling of God are without repentance.' (Romans 11:29, emphasis added)

Therefore Jesus is watching over His gifts as the One responsible for their fulfilment. I am so glad that Jesus Christ is in charge and not men! You can be sure that He will not let you down! Hallelujah!

Other books by Trevor Newport

What the Bible Says About YOUR Provision and Prosperity

Did You Go OR Were You Sent? (An autobiography)

King Jesus Is Coming Soon!

Angels, Demons and Spiritual Warfare

The Ministry of Jesus Christ

Divine Appointments

The Two U's: Unbelief and Unforgiveness

Secrets of Success

From Victory to Victory

Pitfalls in Ministry

How to Pray in the Spirit

The Anointing: the Vital Ingredient

A Practical Guide to Fasting

Prophets, Prophesying and Personal Prophecy

Absolute Faith

As Jesus Is, So Are We in This World

Sharpening Iron: Developing Godly Relationships

Healing, Health and Wholeness

Present Day Miracles